Shelby and the First Ride:

AN OLD QUARRY LAKE FARMS TALE

MARTY KAY JONES

Contents

About The Author

Like Old Quarry Lake's newest resident, Shelby Simone, author Marty Kay Jones grew up obsessed with horses. She also lived in the city and had to wait until her teen years to experience them for herself.

Today, Marty Kay Jones is still obsessed with horses, but now she gets to see them every day. She runs a small boarding stable in the Appalachian foothills and loves teaching new generations everything there is to know about horses.

Ms. Jones believes learning never stops and extends her equine knowledge to readers of the Old Quarry Lake Farms book series. While the books are written about 11-year-old Shelby Simone and her sixth-grade friends, readers of all ages will appreciate and identify with the challenges and triumphs that come with the major life changes Shelby experiences.

When not playing with her own horses, Chip and Mango, Ms. Jones can be found hiking with her Australian Sheep Dog Petey, tinkering around with her project hot rod, or curled up with a good mystery novel.

Exclusive Old Quarry Lake Farms Insider Info

Do you want to join Shelby Simone and her friends from Old Quarry Lake Farms on all their adventures?

Read about Shelby, Katherine, Rose, and all their pals in the Old Quarry Lake Farms Tales book series. Three girls who are wild about horses unite at their local town horse-riding stable. Together, they learn about horses, themselves, and what it means to be a good friend.

The Old Quarry Lake Farms Tales join a group of pre-teen girls who share a bond through horses. Together, they tackle situations like moving to a new town, feeling different, and accepting themselves and each other just as they are—while learning everything they can about horses!

Scan the code to join the Old Quarry Lake Farms email list and never miss out on Shelby's adventures. You'll gain access to bonus material, behind-the-scenes details, and sneak peeks at where Shelby's next steps will take her!

CHAPTER ONE

Introducing Shelby Simone

There had to be something wrong with the clock in Miss Crenshaw's classroom. There just had to be.

It was the last day of school before summer vacation started, and Shelby Simone was absolutely certain that the minute hand was moving slower than ever. What if summer vacation started without her?

It wasn't even like they were learning anything. Miss Crenshaw knew better than to try to teach her fifth-grade class anything on the last day of school, so they were watching a documentary about the United States National Parks. That was cool and everything, but it wasn't as cool as a summer break. Shelby sighed aloud as she looked out the classroom window at the bright sunny day that waited for her.

"Can I help you with something, Miss Simone?" Miss Crenshaw's voice rang out across the classroom. Shelby felt her cheeks burn as they flushed as red as her hair. She hadn't meant to sigh loudly enough for everyone to hear! She shook her head quickly and squeaked out, "No ma'am!"

The class giggled at how high-pitched Shelby's voice sounded. Miss Crenshaw attempted to get control of the class, but Shelby couldn't hear what she said over the pounding of her heart. She felt like her face was turning purple, and it was hard to breathe. That's when Shelby realized she was holding her breath, so she let it all out in a long exhale. *Just breathe, Shelby,* she told herself.

Shelby had a lot of experience being embarrassed. Just looking in the mirror made her feel uncomfortable sometimes. Shelby had inherited her dad's thick, bright red hair, and while it looked good on him, she couldn't help feeling like her hair made her look like some kind of cartoon character.

Plus, she had freckles. And she wore glasses, which most of the kids in her class at Metro School for Girls did not. And to top it off, she was on the chubby side. Even though Metro School for Girls was mercifully devoid of the type of bullies Shelby saw on TV and the Internet, her weight made her an easy target for jokes and jabs. She didn't think the girls really meant to be cruel, but Shelby still felt like she just stood out too much in a crowd—any crowd!

To make matters worse, everyone at school knew about Shelby's obsession. Ever since she could remember, Shelby had loved horses. Not just the coloring books, not just the colorful ponies you could brush, not just the lifelike model horses.

She studied horses. She read every book she could get where there might be a horse. Shelby was in the advanced reading group at school, so she read a lot of both fiction and non-fiction books, all about horses. When Shelby was learning about, reading about, or drawing horses, she didn't feel so embarrassed about herself. She felt like an expert.

Personally, Shelby didn't see what the big deal was. So she knew a lot about horses—so what? Karen Capello was obsessed with soccer, and no one called her Soccer Girl. Adrian Mason was actually in the children's opera, and no one teased her as the Singing Girl. Yet ever since starting kindergarten at Metro School for Girls, Shelby had been Horse Girl. No one was mean about it, but Shelby was just tired of the nickname already. It had been five whole years since Mr. Petersen's class had caught her galloping around the gym and neighing when she thought no one was around!

Shelby's skin prickled the way it only did when somebody was watching her. She realized everyone in the classroom was looking at her. Most of the other girls were trying not to laugh. Her face instantly grew hot again.

"Miss Simone? Honestly, are you alright?" Miss Crenshaw looked a little concerned this time. The teachers at Metro School for Girls called all students "Miss" and it made every question seem that much more severe.

Shelby took a deep breath before she answered, but she made extra-special sure to not breathe too loudly or weirdly before she answered. She didn't want to set the other girls off again. "Yes, Ma'am. I'm sorry. Last-day-of-school-itis." She shrugged meekly.

"Then I suggest you pay attention, as I'm about to announce class is dismissed early! Have a wonderful summer, ladies, and I wish you all the best in sixth grade next year. I've already warned Mrs. Warnerbaker about each and every one of you." Miss Crenshaw waggled her finger teasingly.

It was then that Shelby noticed the growing racket in the halls outside the classroom—excited shouts, promises to stay in touch over the summer, Metro School for Girls' standard-issue uniform shoes squeaking on tiles. The entire school was dismissed early, and because she'd been off in la-la land, she'd almost missed the whole thing. No wonder Miss Crenshaw was concerned. Who dozes off on the last day of school?

Shelby carefully gathered up her things. The building would be locked for the summer, so she couldn't come back if she left her favorite pen behind again. She said goodbye to some of her class buddies and gave Miss Crenshaw a thank you card from her parents. Most of the students at Metro School for Girls gave their teachers presents on the last day. Shelby didn't know what her parents got Miss Crenshaw, but they assured her that it was in the card and that her teacher would love it. She thanked Miss Crenshaw for a wonderful year—and even meant it, mostly—and dashed out into the hallway.

In the hallway, Shelby met up with her friends Amy and Jackie. They had been inseparable since daycare. They all lived in the same condo building just a few blocks away from the school, so they walked together to and from school each day.

They chattered happily as they raced down the school stairs. The Elementary wing of Metro School for Girls was on the second floor of the main building. Next year, the girls would start sixth grade in the Middle School wing, which was across the street. Middle school kids got to walk across the covered sky bridge every day to get to their classes. Shelby and her friends thought that the sky bridge was very cool and couldn't wait to walk across it as big-time sixth graders.

For now, they had to walk on the city sidewalks like regular kids. They scanned out their student ID badges through the front door gates and waited for a crossing guard to escort them across the street, the whole time brainstorming what they would do over summer break.

As usual, Amy had a list of summer movies that she would be dragging Shelby and Jackie to see. Jackie was trying to coax the other two girls into signing up for a junior improv workshop. She was always trying to get the girls to take enrichment courses at the Community Education Center. Shelby had to admit that the art classes had been fun, but she would rather live alone on the moon than try salsa dancing again.

But then Shelby noticed something different. She stopped walking and stared. She could swear that her parents were standing in front of her, but that couldn't be right. They had been working long hours lately, and they hadn't mentioned anything about meeting her at school. Why would they be here? But the faces staring back at her were definitely her mom and dad. And they looked pale and serious.

Amy and Jackie noticed Dr. and Mr. Simone standing there. They said hi awkwardly and dashed off to get snacks at the convenience store on the first floor of their condo building, leaving Shelby alone with her mom and dad.

Shelby's stomach flip-flopped. She got cold and her face flushed. Something terrible must have happened. Maybe Mawmaw fell and couldn't get up! Maybe there had been another national attack! Her heart was racing.

Her parents must have seen the look on her face because her mother stepped quickly to her side. "Oh no, sweetie," she said, putting her hand on Shelby's arm. "It's nothing bad. We have something to talk about, but everything is fine. Even Charlemagne." Shelby's mom knew she was worried about her goldfish without her having to say a word.

"Do you want to go to the park?" Shelby's father stooped a little to talk to her like he was addressing a small child. "Would you like a special snack?"

Shelby's heart was still speeding along, so she couldn't help but grimace. "Oh boy, Dad. That doesn't sound good."

Mr. Simone stood up, chuckling. "Sorry, Old Sport. I guess you're too grown up for park and snacks."

Shelby shook her head. "I love park and snackies, Dad, but I don't think I like where this is going."

"You always have been so perceptive," Dr. Simone sighed. "You're right, Shelby. We have some news, and you're not going to like it. But everyone is okay, and I think you might actually be happy about this in the end." She gave a forced smile to indicate that *of course* everything would be absolutely *splendid*, but Shelby didn't buy it for a second.

"Look, I didn't actually plan to tell you this on the sidewalk in front of your friends, but there's no sense in dragging this out. You know the Old Quarry Lake Project your mom and I have been rambling about the past month?" Shelby's dad continued.

Shelby did. In fact, she felt like she knew more about the Old Quarry Lake Project than most of the people at the museum. Her parents had been fixated on the dig and talked about it all the time.

From what they said, the town of Old Quarry Lake had uncovered a historical location when they were digging to expand the town school. Apparently, they only had one school building for all grades, and it had been getting crowded. When they started building the extension, they found possible evidence of the area being settled several thousand years earlier than they had originally believed.

Dr. and Mr. Simone were anthropologists employed by the Metro Museum of Natural History. Not only was it the largest natural history museum in the state, but it was world-famous. Scientists and researchers came from around the world to study there.

Shelby's parents were experts on ancient Native American civilizations. In fact, they had even appeared on a few television programs to share what they'd learned about different ancient cultures. They had been traveling back and forth from Old Quarry Lake for the past few weeks, so the topic was pretty well discussed at the Simone household.

It was Mr. Simone's turn to grimace. "Here's the thing, Old Sport. That's a two-hour drive each way for us—and that's when traffic is bearable. On Friday evenings, I feel like we're parked on the highway for centuries. Epochs. Eons! I can practically feel myself evolving!"

Dr. Simone cut off her husband. "What we're saying, sweetie, is that it makes more sense for us to actually be based out of OQL. Old Quarry Lake. The town."

Shelby swallowed hard. Had she heard her mother correctly?

Mr. Simone saw the look on Shelby's face and nodded sympathetically. "That's right, Sport. We're moving to the OQL. In a month, so..." he hemmed and chuckled, "I guess you better start packing?"

Dr. Simone gave him a light, scolding tap on the shoulder. "That wasn't funny, Stan," she said. "But he's right. Shelby, we're sorry for the short notice, but we've got to boogie on out of here. We want to give you some time to acclimate to the town before school starts in August."

"Acclimate to the town?" That burst Shelby's shocked silence. "What am I? A sample that needs to be preserved?"

Dr. Simone paused. "You're right. That didn't come out right, and I'm sorry. What I meant is that we want you to have time to meet friends and learn the lay of the land before school gets started. It's one of those small towns where everyone has lived forever, and your father and I figured that giving you the summer to meet people would help your chances of getting along better once school starts. Does that make more sense?"

Shelby nodded. She was feeling shocked, betrayed, resentful, confused, and a little bit like throwing up, but what her parents were saying made sense. In a really awful sort of way, that is.

Shelby started to tear up. She had never felt so completely alone. It was just her now, and it was going to be just her for a while. She was going to live out in what her mother had described as the actual middle of nowhere. She would have no friends. She wouldn't be watching movies or struggling through improv classes with Amy and Jackie. She would be alone.

Mr. Simone cleared his throat. "I promise, it's not all bad, Sport. Your mom and I have taken the liberty of booking you two months of riding lessons at Old Quarry Lake Farms. That's the place you've been talking about, right? The one from the magazines?"

Suddenly, Shelby got very dizzy and sat down abruptly on the warm, filthy city sidewalk.

Shelby's Diary

Oh boy, Diary. Do I have a doozy for you today. I can't believe it.

It's so unbelievable that I almost passed out on the street today. Right in front of the school and everyone!

In the year that I have kept you, Diary, I have never faced anything like this before. I'm so glad Mom showed me how to keep a diary like she does, so I can have a place to write down my thoughts. I'm going to have a lot to think about soon.

We're moving. I have heard kids complain about this a lot—like Ben McKee, whose dad works for the Navy. I know that moving happens, but it wasn't supposed to happen to me!!!!!!!!!! I was just making plans with Amy and Jackie, too. We've never had a summer apart. Ever!!

Now I'm crying, Diary, but I don't really know how to feel. My parents are getting me riding lessons at Old Quarry Lake Farms. THE!!!!!! ONE!!!!! AND!!!!! ONLY!!!!!!!! I was just reading about them on the Midwest Horse Forum. They're rated the best in the region. The owner, Bill Radnor, is a big guy in the barrel world, but they have all sorts of trainers come in, 'cos Bill thinks that horses should be accessible to everyone. Since he's the only big training facility in the area, he makes sure everyone can ride safely and "smartly." His word, not mine.

OMG DIARY. Do country people really say words like "smartly?" OMG. I'm crying again.

Chapter Two

Introducing Old Quarry Lake Farm and Its Folks

"Ok, so, Katherine. Look, I love you, but you and your big lug of a mare need to step up the pace a bit. Whisper and I do *not* have a low drive mode." Rose tossed a quick smile over her shoulder to her friend.

Katherine rolled her eyes. She knew Rose was mostly kidding, but she didn't see why she and her American Quarter Horse mare Comet had to go faster when it was clearly easier for Whisper the tall Thoroughbred to shorten his stride a bit. Plus, she resented Rose calling her horse a "big lug." Quarter Horses were just stocky.

Rose and Katherine had recently picked up a book on traditional gymkhana trials, which had told them all about competitions that tested riding skills and horsemanship. That had almost instantly kicked off a barn-wide fad for timed races and pattern riding. Even though these things weren't taught in regular riding classes, the girls could see the merit in the games. They tested a rider's bond with her horse as well as her skill in staying in the saddle—plus, they were a lot of fun and maybe a little bit dangerous.

For example, the game Rose and Katherine were practicing–or at least *trying* to practice–was called the Toilet Paper Race. Rose was holding a roll of toilet paper, which they had unrolled about five feet. Katherine was holding the other end of the toilet paper. The goal was to ride through a timed course without breaking the toilet paper. That meant they had to ride almost exactly next to each other. The biggest problem, of course, was that Comet was almost two full hands—eight whole inches—shorter than Whisper. There was no way she could keep up with the tall gelding, who was bred for speed.

Katherine adjusted her reins and shook the tension out of her arms. Just then, she heard a booming male voice announce, "DOOR!" The voice belonged to Bill Radnor, owner of Old Quarry Lake Farms, where Rose and Katherine boarded their horses and took weekly riding lessons.

Bill announced his entrance as he opened the arena door so that all of the horses and riders in the arena would be aware that he was coming in. Bill frequently had his horse, Lil' Sugar, in tow, but there was no sign of the little Quarter Horse mare today. Katherine sighed. She could have really used some extra mare power today to silence Rose.

Bill was holding a clipboard and a pen in one hand, and he was fiddling with his phone with the other, muttering as he crossed the arena. "Girls!" he hollered. "Don't make me walk all the way over there!"

Rose and Katherine turned and shuffled their horses over to Bill at a light jog. Bill coughed as he waved dust away from his face. "Yes, and kick up all the arena footing while you're at it. When you girls get done, you need to water this arena. It's like a haboob in here!"

"A what?"

Bill waved his hand, already distracted again. "Look it up."

Katherine nodded. "We'll take care of it, Bill. We're just working on our toilet paper race."

Bill looked from one girl to the other. "Well, good luck with that," he said, chuckling a bit. Rose wrinkled her nose. Just because Bill had been riding forever didn't mean he knew absolutely everything about Gymkhana.

"Practice later, listen up now." He looked flustered, but his smile was still friendly and open. "I wanted to tell you girls about a new student we have coming in. She'll be here in about a month. She's coming in from the city. Never ridden horses before, but her parents tell me she knows everything there is to know about them." Bill paused when Katherine and Rose rolled their eyes. "Now girls, I know what you're thinking, but let's give her a chance. She's about your age, and she doesn't have any siblings, so let's give her the same opportunity y'all had to ride a horse for the first time, OK?"

Katherine wasn't sure what Rose was thinking, but she was thinking about all of the know-it-all city girls who had joined their classes in the past. They called them 3Ds, or "Daughters of Divorced Dads," because these girls were typically accompanied by bored fathers who were trying to win bonus points with their horse-crazy daughters during custodial weekends.

These girls were always the worst. They would refuse to brush their horses because they didn't want to get dirty. Their clothes were super expensive and super clean, and everything was perfectly ironed. But then they would wear some kind of stupid fashion boot instead of an actual riding boot. Rose had once seen a 3D show up in inch-high heels!

The 3Ds treated everyone like servants. They were rude. They didn't even try to ride. They would sit on top of their beloved lesson steed and flop around like feed sacks, then complain that the horse wasn't smooth enough. The girls weren't necessarily mean to the 3Ds, but they sure didn't go out of their way to make them feel included. Rose didn't see any reason to start now.

Rose spoke up first while she and Katherine were watering the arena after Bill left. "I bet this 3D is going to be absolutely clueless. If her parents were bragging to Bill about how much she knows, she must be completely stupid."

Katherine rolled her eyes again. "I know! Horses aren't easy. You don't just Uber a horse." Katherine wasn't entirely sure what an Uber was, but she got the sense that it was some kind of easy delivery thing, which most certainly didn't exist in the horse world—or Old Quarry Lake.

"How long do you think she's going to last?" asked Rose.

Katherine thought about it for a second as she sprayed the corner of the arena. "I bet she doesn't make it through the orientation." Everyone had the same first lesson at Old Quarry Lake Farms, during which Bill would give the new students a tour of the barn, introduce them to the horses, and show them how to groom and tack up before their first ride. Some of the 3Ds gave up the second they learned they'd have to clean stalls.

A voice behind her piped up. "I'll say one lesson!" It was Lisa, another one of the boarders, who had been crossing the arena to get to the other barn. "Hey, Brandi?" Lisa shouted over her shoulder, "What's your bet on the latest 3D?"

Before the barn closed for the evening, all of the young boarders present had placed their dime bets on how long this new 3D would last. Would she run screaming at the sight of a big, muddy, stinky horse, or would she do everyone the favor of falling off epically and hilariously?

Shelby's Diary

Diary, this is it. This is the last time I'll update you in the city. Tomorrow, we head to Old Quarry Lake, or as my parents call it, "The OQL." I don't know if anyone actually calls it that but them.

I said goodbye to Amy and Jackie tonight. We all went out to Mr. Han's Hibachi. Who knows when I'll get to have hibachi again? Mom and Dad told me there isn't any in "The OQL." We had a good time. Mr. Han himself came over to do the shrimp-flipping trick on my plate.

But I could barely eat. Amy and Jackie were busy making plans for the summer. Plans that don't include me! It's like they don't even care that I'm leaving.

On the other hand, Diary, I have way more important things to look forward to!

My mother says that she's already talked to Mr. Bill Radnor, THE owner of THE Old Quarry Lake Farms and that he's excited to meet me. I don't think he really is, but OMG imagine THE Bill Radnor knowing about me! I hope I get to meet him. I'm sure he doesn't actually do stuff in the barn. He's the owner. Like a figurehead. Dad's always talking about how the President of the museum is just a talking head.

Apparently, my first lesson is just a week after we arrive. My mom said unpacking is "Goal Number One"---ugh. I'm so nervous, but it really would be cool if I could meet some horsey friends. Especially since my current friends have already forgotten about me!

It makes my stomach hurt to think about it, Diary, but tomorrow is going to be a big day, so I need to try to sleep.

CHAPTER THREE

Shelby Settles In

Shelby's mom had warned her that life in the OQL was going to be a lot different than life in the city. In fact, both of her parents encouraged her to come with them to the dig site while they were preparing to move so they could check out their new home together. So, while this wasn't her first visit to her new home, she knew there was no return trip to the city. Even Charlemagne was going this time.

Shelby had been hoping that it wouldn't be too different, but as they cruised past the "Old Quarry Lake, Population: 2000" sign that stood at the edge of town, she could see that she had been a little too optimistic.

There were a few similar things. Old Quarry Lake School housed all the grades on one main campus, just like Metro School for Girls. But while MSG took up three buildings on both sides of Broad Street, the school in "the OQL" was just one building.

There was also a downtown area in the rural town. Shelby's dad informed her that it was called "The Square." In the center of the square was a courthouse that somehow combined Greek and Italianate architecture. Shelby knew this because her parents and Miss Crenshaw shared a love of Classical architecture, and Shelby had been trapped in the middle of plenty of their discussions.

Around the courthouse were four streets of shops and restaurants, arranged in an exact geometric square. As if to make things as easy as possible, the four streets were named North Street, South Street, East Street, and West Road. Shelby's parents explained that there was a West Street, but it was built before the courthouse, so they had to name it West Road. Shelby thought this sounded like poor city planning.

The buildings around The Square were built in the late 1800s and early 1900s. Some had businesses on the lower floors and advertised apartments on the upper floors. That made sense to Shelby since there were a lot of places like that in the Old Germantowne section of the city. The businesses themselves were familiar. There was a diner, a florist, a jeweler, a winery, a general store, a theatre, a hotel, an ice cream parlor, and a few places that Dr. Simone said were knick-knacky type stores. Shelby didn't pay attention since she really wasn't interested in shopping.

The town park consisted of a swing set and a slide, along with a picnic shelter and a giant field. Shelby thought that was pretty lame, but on second thought, what was the point of having a park in a town surrounded by so much open space?

There was, in fact, *so much* open space. Shelby remembered going to Wind Cave with her parents a few years ago. Old Quarry Lake wasn't as open as the plains of South Dakota, but everywhere she looked, there was so much nothing.

Maybe *nothing* wasn't the right word. There were hills, valleys, and rolling meadows in every direction, broken up with large thickets of unfamiliar trees. Most of the trees Shelby had encountered in the city were planted strategically along the streets. These grew in unruly clumps with vines and sharp pointy bushes guarding them from human exploration.

The fields were filled with plants Shelby recognized as corn and some kind of bean. She was kind of intimidated by the big open fields, densely planted with rows of crops. She knew where food came from, but she hadn't really appreciated how big farm fields were.

The Simones' new house was located near the school. Shelby's parents decided that once again, Shelby could walk to and from school by herself, or hopefully with her friends, when the time came. Plus, since they would be at the school excavation, she could visit with her parents after school every day.

The house itself was confusing to Shelby, too. In the city, they'd lived in a condo on the seventh floor of a building filled with even more condos. Each floor had a central hallway, with eight doors lining the hallway. Each door opened to another family's condo.

Here, every door opened to more of the same house. It had a bedroom for Shelby, one for her parents, and two spares that were currently filled with boxes of the Simones' belongings. A staircase led to an underground basement, which was finished with wood paneling and bright red carpet that Mr. Simone called excessive, appalling, and ostentatious, and Dr. Simone just called it criminally bad taste.

The house also had a wrap-around front porch that looked out on Broad Street, and if you leaned over the porch railing, you could see the school looming in the not-so-distance. They even had a yard with a huge tree, complete with a tire swing. After a short patch of grass and flowerbeds, the yard abruptly became a cornfield. The cornfield was not theirs, and Shelby's dad warned her not to play in it. Shelby didn't think that would be a problem because she had not realized that corn was very tall and closely planted. In fact, it kind of freaked her out to walk too close to it.

Looking in the opposite direction from the school, Broad Street started to climb a hill, slowly at first, but getting steeper and steeper. If you continued walking up a bit, you could look over the town square. Shelby knew there were kids down there because she could hear them playing in the evening, but so far, she hadn't had a chance to investigate.

One place she had visited was the local tack shop. She had read about tack shops but never had the chance to actually walk in one or breathe in the warm leathery smell she found inside. Tack shops sell supplies for horses, and the one in Old Quarry Lake was attached to the feed store. The feed store sold all sorts of farm goods, from livestock feed and hay to tractor parts. Shelby could identify some of this stuff from her horse books and research, but she was still glad she wouldn't need any of it any time soon. There were a lot of things to know about!

For now, she just needed some paddock boots, a pair of breeches, and a helmet. Bill had explained that the barn had boots and helmets for new riders to try before they spent money on them, but Shelby had insisted that she would want her own. This was her dream. She was going to be riding forever!

Shelby and her mom started with the paddock boots because that seemed like the easiest place to start. Unfortunately, they were wrong. Marian, the helpful lady who owned the tack shop, explained that there are different styles. Did Shelby want lace-up, zip-up, or pull-on boots? Did she want waterproof boots? For riding or mucking?

Shelby's rapidly reddening face must have said everything because Marian stopped asking questions, smiled, and asked Shelby and her mom to follow her. They walked into a small room that was filled with different types of boots. There were paddock boots, alright, but also shiny cowboy boots, clunky steel-toed work boots, rubber mud boots, and boots with big rubber cleats built into the bottom.

Marian smiled again at Shelby and her mom. Her smile was warm and kind, and it was clear she had had this conversation many times before. "First lesson?" she asked. "Which barn?"

"Old Quarry Lake Farms," Shelby squeaked out shyly. Unlike Shelby's classmates, Marian didn't giggle when her voice broke. Instead, she nodded.

"That's where I keep my horse. I think you'll love it there. Bill's a great guy, and he's really involved with his horses and riders. I definitely trust him." She smiled again, even more warmly. "I think you'll love it," she repeated.

For the next few minutes, Shelby, Dr. Simone, and their new friend Marian discussed boots in a dizzying level of detail. First, they established which discipline Shelby would be riding. Many different trainers worked at Old Quarry Lake Farms, teaching different equine sports like English and Western Pleasure, Hunter Jumpers, Barrel Racing, and Reining. Shelby wanted to try everything that could be done on horseback, but she had decided to start out with basic English riding lessons. She liked the way the saddle looked, and she wanted to try jumping someday, which meant starting English riding sooner rather than later.

Shelby was a little embarrassed about sharing these dreams. She knew from reading horse books that jumper riders were very athletic, and well, Shelby was definitely *not*. But she was pretty sure that if she worked really hard towards the goal, she could become athletic enough to ride jumpers. She just wasn't sure what she would need to do yet to get there.

Thankfully, Marian didn't say anything or make a weird face when Shelby shared her dreams. She didn't say anything when she had to fetch Shelby's new breeches out of the women's section instead of the kids' section. They were a little longer than they needed to be for Shelby's height, but Marian very kindly explained that the kids' sizes didn't include Shelby's waist size. Shelby turned bright red again, but Marian said nothing. She only pointed out the elastic-waisted riding tights, which she said she personally found more comfortable than the breeches with a snap waistband. She also showed Shelby how to roll up the cuffs so they wouldn't pinch under her boots.

The helmet part wasn't too painful, either. There were a lot of options to choose from. Some were round while others were oval. Some were cute and colorful, while others were soft black velvet or matte graphite.

Shelby gasped when she saw the price tags on the helmets. Some of them had three zeroes. She had no idea that a helmet was that expensive. Her bike helmet had only cost one week of allowance. This was more like five months of allowance!

When Shelby had finished making her decisions, she and her mother walked up to the counter silently. Shelby started to sweat. She had brought her allowance money, but there were only two zeros in that amount. "M-maybe we don't need the breeches," she stammered.

Dr. Simone stopped in her tracks. "Why do you say that?" She gave Shelby a funny look, and Shelby's heart sank. Did her mother think she'd lost interest in riding lessons? She wanted them more than anything, but she didn't have enough money.

"I only have my allowance with me. I don't know if it's enough." Shelby felt a lump forming in her throat, which meant she was dangerously close to crying.

Dr. Simone only smiled. "Shelby, this is part of the agreement. You can't take two months of riding lessons without the basics."

Marian smiled as well. "Plus, you've chosen some very good, basic equipment that does everything you need without having a big price tag. You're a really smart equestrian shopper. I'm impressed!"

Shelby relaxed a bit. From what Marian said, it sounded like she might just have a knack for this kind of thing. Maybe she was cut out to be a horse person after all.

Shelby's Diary

Diary, the people of Old Quarry Lake are so nice. Everyone knows who we are since we're the only new people who have moved to town in recent history.

I especially like Marian, the lady who owns the tack shop. She helped me find everything I needed. Plus, she carries Dresden model horses, and you know those are my absolute favorite. She's been collecting for 25 years and said she might just let me see some of her best models someday!

Tomorrow is my first riding lesson. I'm not nervous about the horses, Diary. I know what I'm doing there. I know how to curry and pick stalls and the symptoms of laminitis from reading books, but I've never done it before in person.

I just hope I don't embarrass myself. But I REALLY just hope there are kids my age there. Having horsey friends would be so great, especially since Amy and Jackie have been super quiet on our group chat lately. Horsey friends who live nearby and don't ignore me would be ULTI-MATE!

CHAPTER FOUR

Shelby's First Lesson

The gravel crunching under the wheels of Dr. Simone's SUV sounded exactly the way Shelby's stomach felt. As they rolled slowly towards Old Quarry Lake Farms, Shelby felt her face flush and pale alternately, like hot and cold water taking turns running through her veins.

This is it! she thought anxiously to herself. *This is the moment I've waited my whole life for!*

Still, she was filled with just as much dread as excitement. What if she did terribly? What if she fell off? What if she hurt the horse? There were so many things that could go wrong.

Inside the tack room of the barn's front aisle, Katherine and Rose watched a round, bespectacled figure emerge from the rear seat of the SUV. Her unruly red hair was barely contained with a ponytail holder and a headband.

"No way!" said Rose. "There's no way that's the 3D! They aren't usually so..."

"Actually three-dimensional," Katherine finished for her, delicately. It was true that the 3Ds tended to be on the wispy, sleek side, physically speaking.

"Oh, there's no way that girl is ever getting on an actual horse," came Brandi's voice from behind Rose. The other girls of Old Quarry Lake Farms had gathered in the tack room to get the scoop on the new girl.

Outside, Bill Radnor shook hands with Dr. Simone and placed a kind hand on Shelby's shoulder. Through the window, the girls heard him say, "And you must be Shelby! Coins and I have been waiting to meet you. Now if you and your mother could just come with me, we're going to need to sign some stuff, and then I'll show you around. Then," he paused dramatically, "the riding begins!" He winked at Shelby. Shelby looked like she was going to vomit.

As they moved into the barn, Katherine shooed all of the others who had gathered away. Already, they were starting to whisper.

"Did you hear him say she's riding Coins? None of the kids ride Coins. He's for beginner adults."

"It must be because she's so big!"

"I doubt she'll be able to get on him. He's at least fifteen hands high."

With each hand measuring four inches, that meant Coins was sixty inches—or five feet—tall at the base of his neck.

"I don't think she'll even be able to lift the saddle to tack him up!" Katherine was shocked, as these last words had come from Rose.

"Rose!" she scolded. "The new girl may look... different, but you don't need to be mean about it."

Rose frowned. "Yeah, that was a little over the top. But it's not like we're going to have to get used to her being around. It's fine."

And with that, the group scattered around the barn, suddenly busy grooming their horses, picking out stalls, and cleaning their saddles, bridles, and other tack.

Meanwhile, Shelby was feeling a lot better about herself. All of the liability forms for Old Quarry Lake Farms' insurance had been signed, so Bill had allowed Dr. Simone to wander back to her car. She claimed the horses were making her sneezy, but Shelby knew the truth: her mother would rather be anywhere in the world than next to a big, scary, smelly horse.

Bill led Shelby down the six main sections of the barn, labeled A through F. The sections were connected by three different riding arenas. Bill explained that one arena was for general riding, and the others had special footing that made them more suitable for speed events, jumping, and other more intense equine sports. "After all," he said, "the better I take care of these horses, the better they'll be for all of you!"

Shelby liked Bill. He told her right off the bat to drop the whole *Mr. Radnor* thing. "We're all a big family in this group, and we all need to treat each other like equals," he said matter-of-factly. He also explained details Shelby didn't think she needed to know, like what he fed the horses, where they were turned out to graze and roam each day, and how he kept them happy when they were working.

Finally, he stopped at one of the stalls. After passing what seemed like endless stalls filled with glossy black, brown, red, and grey horses, this one was different. The horse standing in this stall was huge and looked more like a clown than a horse. Coins had a short, bristly mane and tail. He was mainly white, but he was also covered in brown and black polka dots.

"This is Coins," Bill said, as he slipped a halter around the horse's nose and fastened it behind Coins' ears. Coins sighed deeply, his nostrils making a "whuffling" noise as the air rushed out.

Bill spoke directly to the horse. "Coins, buddy, I know you don't want to work, but I want you to meet Shelby. She's new here, and this is her first lesson. Are you going to be a good pony for her?" Coins sighed again and licked his lips as if to say "Fine."

Bill noticed Shelby's surprise. "Have you heard of Appaloosa horses? Coins here is a very well-bred Appaloosa specimen."

Shelby had heard of Appaloosa horses. They originated in the American West during cowboy days. Back then they were bred by the Nez Perce Native Americans from the horses that got away from European explorers. Because *Appys*—as they were fondly called—were registered by color and not lineage, they could have stock horse and sport horse lineage. So, they could just as well work the range or compete in nearly every equine sport.

Shelby just hadn't realized how very brightly spotted they could be. Coins had small dots the size of a fingerprint and large dots the size of Shelby's fist. They started at his jaw and went all the way to his tail.

Bill walked the big horse into the aisleway and clipped two long cross ties that hung from the walls to Coins' halter. Shelby got the chance to really assess her noble steed.

Now that he was out of the stall, Coins didn't seem so enormous, but he was pretty tall and muscular. For a few moments, Shelby and Coins simply stared at each other. Bill said nothing and allowed the two to greet each other in their own way.

Around the corner, Rose was sweeping the F aisleway. "She doesn't know what to think. She doesn't even know how to touch a horse," she whispered loudly to Katherine.

Katherine merely rolled her eyes. She had a feeling this 3D wasn't like the others. In fact, she was pretty sure that Shelby wasn't a 3D at all. On the other hand, she really didn't look like the sort of person who would enjoy riding, the way she was staring up at Coins with what Katherine took to be a look of fear frozen on her face.

Bill showed Shelby the curry comb and explained how to use it in a circular motion in the same direction as the horse's hair grew. He then demonstrated how to use a body brush to whisk away the dirt that the curry comb loosened. Shelby snapped out of her trance and groomed Coins like she'd been doing it for years. Then she grabbed the hoof pick without thought and bent over to grab Coins' hoof.

"Whoa there!" Bill put a hand on her shoulder. "Let's go over the basics before you try that one on your own. Coins here is a good boy, but it's really easy to get stepped on– trust me." He pointed to the toes of his boots, which were mashed down and muddy from years of use and abuse.

"What is she doing?" Rose hissed from her observation point. "You don't just pick up a horse's hoof!" Katherine just rolled her eyes and looked for more tasks to do on the other side of the aisle.

Finally, it came time for Shelby to mount up. As if on cue, all of the young riders who had disappeared earlier suddenly reappeared in the doorways, observation rooms, and bleachers surrounding the general riding arena.

Bill showed Shelby how to adjust her girth and stirrup leathers. For her first lesson, she was riding Coins in a basic and comfortable English all-purpose saddle. Bill had attached a long lunge line to the bridle so he could steer Coins from the ground. Since Shelby didn't know how to handle the reins yet, Bill would use the lunge line to encourage Coins to walk in a circle around the trainer.

There was some fiddling of this, tightening of that, a big jump, and suddenly, Shelby discovered she was on top of a horse. She could smell the sweaty, warm scent of Coins, and she felt his rib cage expand under her legs as he breathed. She closed her eyes and let her hands wander down to Coins' soft, spotty neck. This was the moment she had waited for forever. Shelby had found her way to the back of a horse, and she finally felt like she belonged.

Then much to her horror, she realized she was crying. Hot warm tears of happiness were flowing down her face. She needed to pull herself together, of course, but this moment was so amazing. Bill was beaming up at her knowingly, as a trainer who had seen many first-time students fall in love with horses.

But what was that sound? Something like the cawing of birds came from every direction. Shelby opened her wet eyes, confused and a little scared.

That's when she saw them– kids everywhere. Some were young and some were older. They were in the bleachers, inside the barn, even standing outside the door to the walkways between the barns and the pastures. And they were all laughing... laughing at Shelby!

Shelby's Diary

Well, that was 100% enough of that, Diary.

I learned one very important thing today, and that is that I am NOT a horse person. I told Mom and Dad that I was absolutely okay with it if they didn't want me to ride ever again.

I mean, I loved it. I loved it so much. But I was sitting there on Coins—Diary, he is the most beautiful, weird-looking horse I have ever seen—but we were just standing there. STANDING. And I started crying, and everyone was laughing, and I heard someone call me "3D."

Diary... I had to ride the adult horse because the kids' pony was too small for me. I'll never have a pony because I'm too big for a pony. And I'm 3D. Everyone knows I'm too fat to ride. I can't take it.

Bill was very nice. He got everyone to be quiet, and he more or less forced me to walk around on Coins. I stopped crying, obviously, because I was too busy being embarrassed. And then I got too distracted by riding to remember to be embarrassed! Riding is such a weird feeling, Diary. It's like your hips move side to side and front to back at once. And you're just balancing there on your butt with nothing to hang on to!

He told me that it had been a while since they'd had a new student in my age group and to pay the girls no mind, but I knew they were laughing at my weight. I shouldn't have acted like I could just fit in at a barn. These are serious athletes, after all.

Mom says I absolutely have to go to the next lesson, though. She and Dad already paid for it. She said she'll stick with me next time, too. I know that's a big deal for her, but I just wish she could make it easier. If I had parents who LIKED horses, then I'd already be riding now, and I'd be really good, skinny, and pretty, and have tons of friends.

CHAPTER FIVE

Katherine and Rose Feel Terrible

"So, what's this thing about a 3D?" Bill Radnor's face was as kindly as ever, but his words made Katherine's stomach do an unpleasant dance. Rose's face went red and then purple. Giggling about 3Ds with the other girls was one thing, but hearing an adult say it out loud made them feel queasy and embarrassed.

Rose blurted out, "It's a nickname for city kids. The Daughters of Divorced Dads. 3Ds. It's not supposed to be mean. They're just what we call those rich city girls who only come in for one lesson. And they think they know everything, and they talk down to us, and it's really just unpleasant..." Rose trailed off and glanced at Bill and Katherine nervously.

Katherine tried very hard not to roll her eyes. While she admired Rose's honesty and bravery, sometimes she "speaks, when silence would suffice," as Katherine's mother put it.

Bill took a deep breath and nodded. The girls had never seen him so solemn, and this different side of Bill was making them feel very anxious. When he had asked them to talk in the quiet end of Aisle B, they had immediately become a little nervous. This was the worst-case scenario level.

"So, Shelby, the new girl, who is not a 3D, but a new resident of our fine town, along with her parents—her married parents, mind you—heard all of you whispering and giggling and thought you were picking on her about her weight."

"We would never!" Rose heard herself cry, but then she clamped her mouth tightly. They *had* made comments about the new girl's weight, though. Rose hadn't thought they were being mean, but they hadn't really said anything nice. Besides, Shelby and her body weren't any of their business.

Bill seemed to see right through Rose, but he continued. "Anyhoo, when Shelby arrives for her lesson in a while here, it would be just swell if you could avoid making her feel uncomfortable. I won't force you to apologize to her because I reckon she'd be pretty embarrassed if she knew I was having this conversation with you." He chuckled, "I may be old in your eyes, but I know enough about being awkward and nervous. Especially in those teenage years."

He made his way towards the main arena. "But if you see fit to try to make things right with Shelby, I can see how that would make her joining the Old Quarry Lake Farms family a little more comfortable."

By the time the girls watched Shelby's mother drop her off at the barn about an hour later, the overall mood had changed at Old Quarry Lake Farms. Katherine and Rose had spent their time raking and sweeping the aisleways, brainstorming what they could do to apologize to Shelby. True, 3D didn't mean what she thought, but the girls had been making fun of her appearance all the same.

Plus, it was kind of obvious that Shelby hadn't been crying because she was scared. The kids who were terrified didn't sit still or close their eyes. Sometimes they didn't even breathe! Shelby had looked... "blissed out," as Katherine put it.

Meanwhile, Shelby entered the barn as slowly as she had exited her mother's car. She wasn't too enthusiastic about her lesson. Bill wasn't anywhere to be seen, either. Maybe he had forgotten. Maybe Shelby could just spend the next hour in the view room, reading the stacks of horse magazines kept in there and munching on the granola bar her mother had packed her as a snack. She peeped her head into the view room to scope out the situation.

The view room was so named because it had a large window looking out across the general riding arena. It was the main hangout space for riders and parents alike. Inside, there was a kitchenette space with a refrigerator, microwave, and coffee pot. There was a private bathroom, a table and chairs, and a couple of tattered and dusty recliners. On each recliner was a heating pad, plugged in and ready to soothe sore legs and bottoms—or cold parents in the winter.

Shelby could see Bill in the arena. He was riding a small dark brown horse. Shelby was astonished at how small the horse really was, yet she was dashing around the arena with absolute grace. Like Shelby, Bill was on the heavier side. Yet here he was, seeming to float around the arena with this tiny little horse.

Bill brought the mare to a walk and motioned for Shelby to come to the arena door. She closed the view room door and walked around the corner to the main arena door, being sure to shout "DOOR" as Bill had taught her.

Bill and the little mare sauntered up to her. "Shelby, I'd like you to meet Lil' Sugar, the best-darned barrel horse that ever was or has been."

Shelby stared up at the horse. "Please to meet you, Lil' Sugar," she said, as she gave her a pat on the neck. Lil' Sugar gently sniffed at Shelby, making a soft *woofle* noise.

"I know your last lesson was a little rough. I've talked to the girls about making a fuss during your lesson. Now don't get all embarrassed. I'm the one who chose to talk to them because I heard them giggling and causing a ruckus, and that's not the type of family we have here at my farm. They've informed me that their comments had nothing to do with your physical appearance."

Shelby immediately blushed. She wanted to disappear at the mention of her weight. But Bill continued.

"I know it's not easy, but I want to see if we can *not* focus on last time today. Instead, let's get you up on Coins, and have a brand new, great, totally different ride. Does that sound like something we can do?"

Shelby looked up at Bill and Lil' Sugar. They made such a great team, and she and Bill had been absolutely dancing around the arena earlier. Shelby wanted to experience that more than anything in the world.

She nodded enthusiastically, taking a deep breath as she did so. "Yes. Let's do it!"

Bill smiled. "I was hoping you'd say that. Now, I need to cool Miss Thing out here, but if you give me a couple of minutes, we can get Coins ready. Go ahead and hang out in the view room if you like."

As Shelby made her way back to the arena door, Bill shouted over his shoulder. "Oh, and Shelby, don't worry about this." Bill gestured with one hand at his entire body, which was a little on the pudgy side. "Look at me. We're all built differently, horses and people alike. We all look different ways and do different things. Folks like us just need to make sure we find horses that can pair up with us. Like Lil' Sugar here. You wouldn't expect her to drag around a guy like me, but she's built like steel. You just gotta find what works. You just keep showing up and riding and learning. I'll make sure you're on the right horse until you're ready to choose one on your own."

And suddenly, Shelby burst into the biggest grin she had ever grinned. Maybe she was a horse person, after all.

Shelby's Diary

Diary, I have had pretty much the best day ever. I can't believe it.

I went to my riding lesson, even though I really didn't want to. Mom dropped me off because she had to get back to the dig site, or so she said. I think she just didn't want to be around horses again. Remember how she said she would stick with me during my lesson, Diary? I guess I was disappointed, but not surprised. She did take me out for a super-nummy grilled cheese at the diner when she picked me up and apologized a hundred times, but that's not even the best part of this story.

Diary, I am a horse person. Bill and I had the longest, most awkward conversation about the girls who laughed at me and weight and body stuff. Bill's bigger, like me, but he has the most amazing horse. Her name is Lil' Sugar. She's a ten-year-old dark bay Quarter Horse mare, and she looks so small. But she's in great shape and muscled up, so she can carry Bill around with no problem. She's also a National Champion in barrel racing! And I got to pet her! She's so sweet.

During my lesson, Bill and I talked about the muscles that people use when riding, and how I'll naturally build strength there as I keep riding. And I'm going to keep riding, Diary. No joke! When no one else was around, and it was just me and Bill and Coins, it was so amazing.

But here's the best part. After my lesson, two of the girls I saw last week came up to me. Their names are Katherine and Rose, and they've been riding at Old Quarry Lake Farms forever. Katherine's horse is named Comet, and Rose's horse is Whisper.

Anyway, they wanted to tell me that they were sorry for disrupting my lesson. Rose also told me what 3D means. It stands for Daughters of Divorced Dads and has nothing to do with my weight. Or anyone's weight, for that matter. Rose said she's glad my parents are still married, which was a little weird, but I think she was just feeling super awkward. I know I did.

Katherine and Rose are going to be starting 6th grade next year, too. They asked me if I wanted to hang out next week after my lesson. I asked my mom, and she said sure! They're going to take me "around town" so I can learn more about "the OQL." I really need to find out if they actually call it that, too.

CHAPTER SIX

The Best Summer Ever

S helby's mother gazed at her daughter with a mixture of impatience and affection. "I understand you're excited, sweetie. I swear, you look fine. Your friends are going to love the snacks we got. And if they don't... I really think you might have to look for new friends. Who doesn't love nachos?"

Shelby just wanted everything to be perfect. After a week of hanging out with Katherine and Rose at the barn and around town, she had finally invited them and their families to her home. Dr. and Mr. Shelby were excited to meet Shelby's new friends and had helped her prepare snacks for them to share.

While the adults got to know each other, the girls decided to watch footage from the World Equestrian Games that Rose had found on YouTube. She said she'd discovered links to all of the disciplines. Maybe that would help Shelby decide what she wanted to do with her riding future. After all, she was a horse person now!

The past week had been so much fun. Katherine and Rose had taken Shelby to the arcade, the ice cream parlor, and the general store, where a person could still get root beer barrel candy for a dime. Shelby had never had a root beer barrel before but fell in love with its sticky, herby sweetness.

Most of the time they hung out at the barn, doing odd jobs for Bill like raking the aisleway and watering the arenas. They also spent plenty of time grooming, playing with, and plain old spoiling Comet and Whisper. Shelby was anxious for the day she could have her own horse, but she knew she wasn't ready just yet.

As she waited for her friends and their families to arrive, Shelby was beyond nervous. It felt like the butterflies in her tummy had their own butterflies. Shelby was going to introduce her new friends to her inner world. Granted, that was just her mom and dad, but she'd never introduced friends to her parents before. Amy and Jackie had grown up knowing the Simones since they were born.

Just then, there was a knock at the door. Shelby whirled around to open it. She'd been standing in the hallway waiting for just this moment! Rose was accompanied by her parents, whom Shelby hadn't met yet. Mr. Jensen was the Sheriff of Old Quarry Lake, and he had apparently already met Dr. and Mr. Simone. He gave Mr. Simone a big handshake as he entered and introduced Mrs. Jensen. Mrs. Jensen had her hands full with Rose's siblings. Peony and Jacob were two-year-old twins. Rose claimed they were well-behaved for kids that age. As an only child, Shelby had no way to tell, but they were awfully cute as they sat in a side-by-side stroller Mrs. Jensen had strapped them into. Like the rest of the family, the Jensen twins had strawberry-blonde hair and big blue eyes.

Katherine and her family were close behind the Jensens, so all three families gathered on the Simones' large wrap-around porch. Katherine's parents were both doctors at the Marble County Hospital. "Since my parents are both doctors, they're both technically 'Dr. Wilson,'" Katherine had explained to Shelby. "So, you can call my dad Dr-Mr. Wilson and my mom can be Dr-Mrs. Wilson."

Also tagging along was Katherine's older brother Drew. Drew was technically a junior in high school, but he was about to start attending classes at the Marble County Community College, which was near the hospital where the Wilsons worked. Shelby had met Drew at the barn since he was responsible for driving Katherine around while their parents were at work. She and Katherine were secretly hoping Shelby's parents would let Drew drive Shelby around, too, so she could get more horse time. They were trying to figure out how to bring up the subject later that night.

After the Simones introduced themselves to the Jensens and the Wilsons, the girls broke off to go do what Drew jokingly called horse nerd stuff.

"Whatever," Katherine said with a roll of her eyes. "You just keep texting your AI girlfriend."

"It's an app I'm beta testing!" the girls heard Drew shout behind them. Soon they were gathered around the computer in the Simones' den.

"We can watch the show footage on the big TV, but it's really old and grainy," Shelby explained. "Dad's computer monitor is super-mega-ultra-high-def." She blushed a little. She didn't want to sound like she was bragging. "He has to look at a lot of scans and photos and videos and stuff like that for work."

Rose nodded. "I totally get it. Dad has a work tablet that is so clear, you can see the freckles on a suspect's..." She paused. "Face."

Katherine also voted for the super-mega-ultra-high-def screen. She loved being able to take in every detail of the rider's turnout and tack, or the clothing and equipment they used in the show ring. She secretly wanted to be a professional rider but logically knew that she would need to work pretty hard to get to that level. In the meantime, she could watch, learn, and covet the special—and expensive!—equipment the pros had.

Shelby looked around at the girls and flushed. "I don't mean to sound like a jerk, but could you put your drinks on the table over there?" She pointed to the coffee table in front of the television and sofa. "I just don't want to screw up Dad's computer." She flushed even deeper and hastily apologized. "Not that I think you would. I just mean that…"

Katherine cut her off. "No worries," she reassured Shelby. "We keep liquids and devices separate at my house, too. Try living with doctors. Everything is a risk."

Rose chuckled. "I'm used to hiding things from toddlers. Just watch that I don't put stuff on a higher bookshelf or something!"

Shelby exhaled, relieved. It was so nice to have friends who understood her. "Thanks, guys. So which event do we want to start with?"

"If we don't start with show jumping, I will actually riot," Rose said quickly.

"If we don't get to watch at least a few dressage tests, I will also riot," Katherine added. "But I think we should watch show jumping first."

And so, the girls gathered around Mr. Simone's fantastic computer monitor to watch equine and human athletes hurdle over huge jumps at incredible speeds. Just a month ago, Shelby had only dreamed of knowing what that would be like. Now she knew what riding a horse on the walk felt like. Going that fast and jumping that high seemed terrifying, but a small part of her still wanted to try it, too.

A loud laugh from upstairs seemed to say that the adults and Drew were having a good time, too. Rose rolled her eyes. "My dad's laugh is SO annoying!"

But Shelby didn't mind at all. In fact, she had never been more content.

Shelby's Diary

Seriously, Diary, can you believe everything that has happened in the past month? Ok, I guess it's been just over a month. But still.

It seems just like yesterday that I was trying not to pass out on Broad Street during the after-school rush. Hey Diary, remember that time my parents told me we were moving? In public? Outside? LOL Now I have to keep my boots outside on the mud porch because Dad thinks they smell too much like horse manure.

The Wilsons and the Jensens came over last night. That's Katherine and Rose's families. The parents got to meet. Katherine and I were going to ask if Drew could take me to the barn when Katherine goes, but apparently, our parents thought it was a great idea before we could even talk to them about it. Looks like I'm going to be spending more time getting my boots stinky, Diary!

It's still weird to think that I lived in the city just over a month ago. I talked to Amy and Jackie in our group chat the other day. Jackie got Amy to sign up for improv and mime, so they've been too busy to talk.

I thought I was really going to miss them. I guess I do. But they haven't been really talking in the group chat, and I guess I've been talking more to you and horse people than my city friends. Mom and Dad said I could invite them out to visit us, but apparently, they have four more weeks of improv and mime, and then they're going to their vacation houses in the Florida Keys. "As per usual," Jackie wrote, LOL

Anyway, there's something about being out here in Old Quarry Lake that feels more comfortable than I felt in the city. At first, it was weird not to hear traffic and horns honking all night. Plus, frogs make really weird noises. But I'm used to it now. I have friends here. I ride horses here. At least, I think Old Quarry Lake is starting to feel like home.

OH YEAH. PS, Diary– No one calls it "The OQL" except my dad. Well, Sheriff Jensen might start calling it that. I asked about it when all the families were over. Dad admitted he made it up because it sounded like an airport call signal. Good grief. There's no airport in Old Quarry Lake, or Marble County at all! Anyway, Sheriff Jensen thought that was hilarious and kept calling it "The OQL" all night. I hope he forgets about it soon or my new friends are going to think my family is weird.

"My friends" sounds so cool. My new horsey *friends, Diary. And we're going to spend all summer doing horsey things together before school starts again. And then we're going to do horsey things after school. It's going to be a horsey summer. The one I've always dreamed of!*

Review

Reviews and feedback help improve this book and the author. If you enjoy this book, we would greatly appreciate it if you could take a few moments to share your opinion and post a review on Amazon. Thank you!

Exclusive Old Quarry Lake Farms Insider Info

Do you want to join Shelby Simone and her friends from Old Quarry Lake Farms on all their adventures?

Read about Shelby, Katherine, Rose, and all their pals in the Old Quarry Lake Farms Tales book series. Three girls who are wild about horses unite at their local town horse-riding stable. Together, they learn about horses, themselves, and what it means to be a good friend.

The Old Quarry Lake Farms Tales join a group of pre-teen girls who share a bond through horses. Together, they tackle situations like moving to a new town, feeling different, and accepting themselves and each other just as they are—while learning everything they can about horses!

Scan the code to join the Old Quarry Lake Farms email list and never miss out on Shelby's adventures. You'll gain access to bonus material, behind-the-scenes details, and sneak peeks at where Shelby's next steps will take her!

Please join My Facebook group

https://www.facebook.com/MartyKayJones/

https://www.facebook.com/groups/881663880022320/

Made in United States
Troutdale, OR
09/08/2024

22686144R00030